THE MARTINI

Also by Matt Hranek

The Negroni

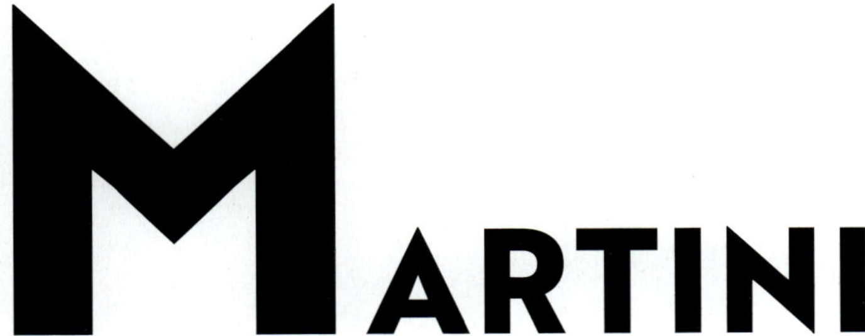

PERFECTION IN A GLASS

MATT HRANEK

NEW YORK

Library of Congress Cataloging-in-Publication Data

Names: Hranek, Matt, author.
Title: The martini / Matt Hranek.
Description: New York, NY : Artisan, a division of Workman Publishing Co., Inc. [2021] | Includes index.
Identifiers: LCCN 2020056675 | ISBN 9781579659639 (hardcover)
Subjects: LCSH: Martinis. | LCGFT: Cookbooks.
Classification: LCC TX951 .H729 2021 | DDC 641.87/4—dc23
LC record available at https://lccn.loc.gov/2020056675

Design by Headcase Design
Photographs by Matt Hranek, except as noted on page 157.

Published by Artisan
A division of Workman Publishing Co., Inc.
225 Varick Street
New York, NY 10014-4381
artisanbooks.com

Printed in China on responsibly sourced paper

10 9 8 7 6 5 4

To all the bartenders who have
served me a perfect martini

for the best
Cocktail...
The name to remember
when you want a Martini
RENFIELD IMPORTERS, LTD., N.Y.
MARTINI & ROSSI
IMPORTED EXTRA DRY VERMOUTH

CONTENTS

Question:
With so many fine gins around
why choose Bombay?
Answer:
Read
our label.
IMPORTED FROM ENGLAND
BOMBAY
DISTILLED LONDON
DRY GIN
Distilled from
100% Grain Neutral Spirits
FROM A 1761 RECIPE
86° Proof 4/5 Qt
Bombay Spirits Co., Ltd., London, England
Sole Distributors for U.S.A.
CARILLON IMPORTERS LTD.
New York, N.Y.
Product of England
THERE'S ONLY ONE
WORLD'S FINEST
BOMBAY
IMPORTED ENGLISH GIN
DISTILLED AND BOTTLED IN ENGLAND
WHAT IS GIN?
Gin is a state of mind. But, Gin is a recipe . . . Gin is Bombay. There's Only One World's Finest.
No two Gins are the same because Gin is a recipe. Certain English Gins have the flavor distilled in. The flavor of Gin makes the drink. The flavor of a true English Dry Gin is acquired in distilling from "botanicals." In distilling, as the vapor is boiled off it rises through racks of selected natural flavoring agents. These are:
1. Coriander (seeds) from Morocco
2. Lemon Peel from Spain
3. Angelica (root) from Saxony
4. Licorice from England
5. Orris (Iris flower) from Italy
6. Juniper (berries) from Germany
7. Almonds from Indo-China
From all of these Bombay Gin acquires that very slight, elusive flavor that makes Bombay a true, distinctive, dry Gin. This entire distilling process is further enhanced by a method of unhurried distillation which ensures that there is only one world's finest.

PREFACE

At this point in my adult life, drinking resembles a day at the track. It's a thoroughbred race of sorts—fast out of the gate, followed by a mad dash to a quick buzz—rather than an all-day marathon of sipping one beer after another toward a long, slow burn.

Life is short, and time feels of the essence. My tastes, metabolism, and schedule have changed since my college days. I don't have the time or inclination to dillydally, and all that beer no longer appeals to me (or my waistline).

Thankfully, I have fallen in love with the martini (or the "marty," as we call it in my house), which consistently has me off and running with speed, elegance, and style. En route from one place to the next, I follow the silhouette of a martini glass (the international symbol for cocktail) on signage throughout any airport just before a flight.

My father drank his gin with tonic, so my early exposure to the martini was mostly through cinema. Hollywood has always loved the martini, casting it in a supporting role in countless classic movies, from those directed by Billy Wilder to any of the Bond films.

I started ordering martinis when I could first afford them, shortly after moving to New York City in the early 1990s, as a way to look sophisticated on dates. Since I favored places where martinis were served very dry (read: mostly gin) in oversize (10-ounce/300 ml+) glasses, just one got me feeling confident quite quickly (read: cheap date). The martini soon became one of my go-to cocktails—the Negroni being the other.

My most memorable martini was at Temple Bar on Lafayette Street. The bar felt like an elegant yacht interior: dimly lit, with interior: dimly lit, with dark-wood walls and heavy velvet curtains. They served popcorn with crisp shreds of fried sweet potato and beet at the bar—very salty, to encourage more drinking. The martini glasses were big, chilled, and filled to the brim with the coldest and driest of drinks. There was a sense of glamour and fun surrounding Temple Bar (and the martinis) that I just had to be a part of.

Dating back to the mid-nineteenth century, the martini is one of the world's most popular cocktails—and with good reason. It is sophisticated, evocative, and delicious. Making a martini is simplicity itself, requiring just two (not counting the garnish) basic ingredients: gin and vermouth. No special tools or expertise are required. After an especially taxing day, there is perhaps no greater pleasure than mixing and sipping a cold one. It announces that the day is over and you have earned your drink, the reward for a job well done.

As with the Negroni, the origin of the martini is steeped in mystery and intrigue, with more than a few unverified theories as to how and where it came to be. Some claim the martini was invented in (and named for) the town of Martinez, California (see page 46 for the namesake recipe), while others credit Martini & Rossi for coining the name of the drink. Other aficionados attribute it to a San Francisco bartender named Jerry Thomas, while some point to New York City—specifically the Knickerbocker Hotel—as home to the very first martini. Honestly, since I'm never as interested in the drink that came first as I am in my next one, this book will not waste your time exploring and debating the competing origin stories. Rather, it celebrates the martinis I have come to love over the years, and the places I have discovered in which to best enjoy them.

There is not one proper martini recipe, per se. For me, the ideal martini is made with gin, served ice cold and bone-dry, with a twist. By definition, a martini includes gin, and it should not need to be qualified as such. A vodka martini is just that—a variation on the original. The use of the term "gin martini" is a retronym, a phrase created to avoid confusion between

the standard and a later version. (Similar phrasing is used to describe an "acoustic guitar," for example, or an "analog watch.")

Occasionally I've been served a lousy martini, but that hasn't deterred me. When one is prepared with thought and care, there is nothing closer to perfection in a cocktail. I have tasted martinis in countless airport bars, hotels, and restaurants, crafted by bartenders all over the globe. I have also heard tell of various well-known figures who love the martini as much as I do, from President Franklin Delano Roosevelt to the writer Dorothy Parker, each pontificating on the glories of this iconic drink. Ultimately, I identify most with the following assessment, from Homer Simpson, in reference to his favorite bartender: "He knows just how I like my martini—full of alcohol."

Frank Sinatra and Jill St. John in Tony Rome, *1967*

THE COMPONENTS

THE MARTINI IS AS SIMPLE as it is sophisticated. Because you need just a few ingredients to mix one, it's worth seeking out excellent examples of each, and combining them with the right amount of care. You have a bit more license with your choice of garnishes, the best of which offer a sharp, crisp counterpoint to the gin—a bright twist of lemon peel, say, or a bracing, briny olive. If you are new to the drink, experiment to see what you like best. Or, if you're like me, you might switch gears depending on the place and situation you find yourself in.

THE

GIN

The key to the martini's flavor is its primary component, the gin (or, more specifically, the juniper that gives it its name). The spirit originated in the Netherlands, as a variant of genever (sometimes spelled jenever, which comes from the Dutch word for juniper).

The earliest versions of genever were crudely distilled from malt wine. These primitive spirits were definitely rougher around the edges than modern-day gins, bearing more resemblance to whiskey, though not quite as palatable. They needed some polishing, so distillers added botanicals and herbs to increase their appeal, taking an especially generous hand with the juniper.

Since juniper was thought to have healing properties, early genevers (from about the sixteenth century) were used medicinally. British soldiers battling wars in the Netherlands around that time discovered the spirits and developed a taste for them. They brought genever back to England with them, and the British public soon developed a taste for it too. Once its popularity was established, English distillers began producing their own version of genever, altering its composition and shortening the name to "gin." Eventually they created a clear, more smooth grain alcohol than the Dutch original, with a pronounced juniper flavor. Today, we know this as London dry gin, my unequivocal choice for a martini.

Some cocktail historians claim Old Tom–style gin as the spirit of choice in early versions of the martini (see page 46). This variety is something of a halfway point between the somewhat primitive genever-style gins and the ultra-dry London-style varieties we know today. Old Tom gins were made when most gin was still relatively harsh, prompting distillers to mellow the effect with sugar and other sweeteners, including licorice.

In the middle of the twentieth century, as the preference for sweetness in popular cocktails gave way to one for dryness, Old Toms fell out of favor. However, you can still find Old Tom gins made by distillers such as Hayman's. In some circles, you can even find martini lovers who prefer their drinks decidedly less dry, but Old Tom–style gin has always been too sweet for my palate. I favor the piney and soft citrus notes of London dry gin, as well as the complexity of the botanicals and the rooty finish. I would never opt for a flavored gin, like one that is lemon- or cucumber-infused, in my martini, lest it cloud the purity of the drink. There are currently many great producers of London dry gins all over the world—now more than ever, in fact. My go-to gin choices include the following:

- Beefeater
- Berry Bros. & Rudd No. 3
- Bombay
- Botanist
- Gordon's
- Monkey 47
- Plymouth
- Tanqueray

There are loads of other gins from small-batch producers that I like to try when I come across them. When I'm in Brooklyn, for example, I'll often opt for one of the local favorites, like Dorothy Parker or Brooklyn gin. When I'm in upstate New York, I'll buy Prohibition gin.

GIN
It's got to be Gordon's

THE VERMOUTH

In a classic martini, the vermouth is always dry. Also known as white (blanc or bianco) vermouth or French vermouth, this blond barrel-aged fortified wine was developed in France in the early nineteenth century by brands like Noilly Prat (distillery pictured below) and Dolin. Author W. Somerset Maugham put it best, as quoted in a vintage advertisement: "Noilly Prat is a necessary component of a dry martini. Without it, you can make a sidecar, a gimlet, a white lady, or a gin and bitters, but you cannot make a dry martini."

Dry vermouth is not to be confused with (or substituted for) its sweet red counterpart, which has an entirely different flavor profile. Both varieties were originally intended for medicinal purposes, and infused with an array of botanicals and flavoring agents. It's the blend of those ingredients and the proportions in which they are used that continue to give each dry vermouth its signature character and taste.

The exact formula for any commercial vermouth is a highly guarded secret, but all brands generally include a bitter plant or root (such as wormwood, or *wermut* in German, the shrub that accounts for the spirit's name). Among other typical flavorings are citrus peels, flowers, herbs, leaves, and spices such as nutmeg, coriander, cinnamon, allspice, and cloves. (Unlike dry vermouth, sweet vermouth includes sugar and other sweeteners, along with coloring agents to produce its red hue.) My go-to vermouths (dry and sweet) are:

- Antica Formula
- Carpano Dry
- Dolin
- Martini (in a pinch)
- Noilly Prat
- Punt e Mes

THE BITTERS

Like vermouth, aromatic bitters (also known as cocktail or tincture bitters) were developed for medicinal purposes; they too were steeped with herbs and spices, tree bark and roots, and dried fruit. Unlike vermouth, however, bitters were based on high-proof alcohol rather than wine. These cure-alls and tonics were used primarily to treat stomach ailments.

Aromatic bitters are not to be confused with Italian bitters, the aperitifs and digestifs (think Campari and amaro) that you're likely to enjoy in cocktails like the Negroni. Because aromatic bitters are extremely potent (and, well, bitter), a dash or a drop is usually all you need to flavor a martini or other cocktail. Bitters were added to the Martinez (page 46), an early version of the martini, way back in 1849, and they are included in one of my favorite modern riffs on the classic, the Martini Twist (page 61).

Cocktail bitters can be found in small bottles in many supermarkets and most liquor stores. A few of the more widely available brands were developed by nineteenth-century doctors and pharmacists. Angostura, for example, is named for the town in Venezuela where the company's founder, Dr. Johann Siegert, worked as surgeon general to Simón Bolívar's army. Peychaud's was created by Antoine Amédée Peychaud, a Creole apothecary who settled in New Orleans, where his bitters gained fame as a key component of the Sazerac, the city's favorite cocktail. Fee Brothers, another popular brand of bitters, has been produced by the same family in upstate New York for four generations.

For the special people who know the difference...

STOLICHNAYA

(Stōl-itch-naya)

the only vodka imported from Russia

The only vodka produced and bottled in Russia distilled of grain neutral spirits and imported at 80 and 100 proof by Monsieur Henri Wines Ltd., New York

THE VODKA

To me, gin defines the martini. The gin in all the recipes in this book can be replaced with vodka, if you are so inclined, but as I've stated here, I prefer gin in my martini. It was the original spirit and, as such, delivers the intended flavor and character of the iconic cocktail. Although gin and vodka are technically the same distillate, I stick to the juniper-forward, botanical notes of the classic version.

That said, when it comes to vodka, I like Tito's for its discernible flavor (I want my distilled spirits to actually taste of something). I'm also partial to old-school Russian vodkas such as Stolichnaya, as well as anything Polish.

THE GARNISH

Since the components of a proper martini are so few, one way to customize your cocktail is with the garnish. Olives or citrus twists are the most common, followed by cocktail onions. Ultimately, the choice is up to you.

OLIVES

There is something nostalgic and cool about a martini with a pimento-stuffed olive (the supermarket jarred variety). One olive per drink is the norm. I like the aesthetic and the savory kick that one olive brings to a martini, and if I'm hungry, I might choose that over my standard lemon garnish. I always opt for a pitted or stuffed olive, preferably from the Musco Family Olive Co. Add a few more olives (along with some of the brine), and you have a dirty martini (see page 135). Or drop a large blue cheese–stuffed olive into your martini for the so-called filthy version (see page 139).

CITRUS

Lemon peel will always be my go-to garnish in a martini. I like its bright, clean, unobtrusive nature. Use a vegetable peeler or a sharp knife to remove a wide swath of the peel, pressing lightly to avoid picking up any of the bitter white pith. If you see a lemon peel described as "expressed," that means the strip of peel has been squeezed over the cocktail to release the oil before it garnishes the drink; it might also be rubbed around the rim of the glass before it's dropped into it.

A twist is made by removing a thin strip of peel with a vegetable peeler or a knife, working your way around the fruit to remove one long, continuous piece. If you feel like it (and have the time), you can tie one of these long pieces into a knot as a variation. Substitute other citrus fruits, like lime, orange, or grapefruit, in place of lemon if that is your preference. Dukes Bar in London uses a twist of organic orange peel in its Vesper martini (see page 116).

COCKTAIL ONIONS

Cocktail onions are the classic garnish for a Gibson (page 79), but they can be used in place of olives or citrus peel in a classic martini, as well. The tiny pearl onions, which are sweeter than larger onions, are peeled and pickled in spiced brine. You can find jarred cocktail onions in any supermarket, and these should serve you well in most cases. If you want to pickle your own, by all means do so. Pickled ramps (a wild allium that grows in upstate New York and elsewhere in the spring) are my favorite variation on the cocktail onion garnish. (See page 82 for the recipe.)

MARTINI ROSS
ORDON'S
ISTILLED
NDON DRY
GIN

THE EQUIPMENT

OTHER THAN A SPIRIT or two, some ice, and your garnish of choice, you won't need much to put together a memorable martini. Here are some tips on the tools you'll need for measuring, mixing, chilling, and garnishing your cocktails, plus recommended glassware for serving and drinking them.

BARWARE

All the items in the list that follows are found in any standard bartender's arsenal (and in many home kitchens too).

JIGGER

Use a jigger to measure the ingredients for a martini if you're new to mixing your own or happen to be a stickler for precision. You can find jiggers in a variety of materials and myriad styles, from elegant and ornate to simple and utilitarian. Truth be told, I usually measure by eye, but I do keep a few jiggers on hand for others.

BAR SPOON

A bar spoon serves two purposes when making a martini: The long handle is essential for the "stirred, not shaken" method (see page 36), and the spoon serves as a measure (about 1 teaspoon/5 ml) for ingredients such as vermouth. Keep yours in the freezer for the iciest chill.

STRAINER

A well-made short-handled bar strainer shouldn't cost much, and it's designed specifically for cocktail prep rather than for use in cooking.

VEGETABLE PEELER

Professionals may use the tool called a channel knife to remove citrus peel, but I've always found that a standard vegetable peeler suffices. Starting at the top of the fruit, use a light hand to work your way around it, moving from top to bottom. Aim for evenly thick strips roughly 3 inches (7.5 cm) long. You want to avoid pressing too hard, lest you pick up any of the bitter white pith. (If you do end up with some pith, simply scrape it off the colored part of the zest with a sharp knife.)

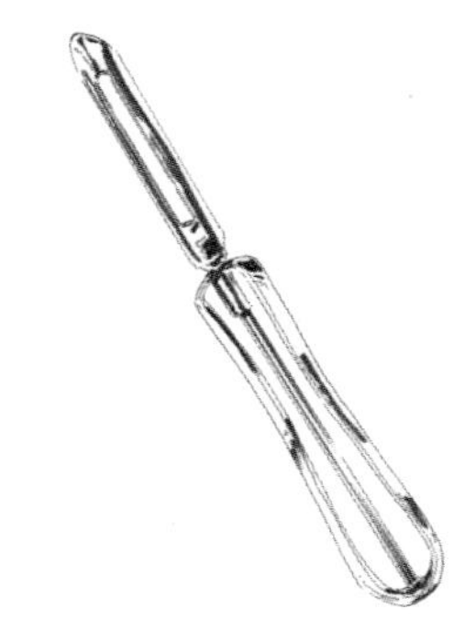

MIXING GLASS AND COCKTAIL SHAKER

Depending on your preferred method, you'll put one of these two bar essentials to good use. It's worth having one of each so that you can mix drinks for guests too, per their own preferences. Stainless steel is the material of choice for bartenders. For the home bar, options for mixing glasses abound, from the finest Baccarat crystal to repurposed glass jars. Don't overthink it: Use whatever you have on hand.

GLASSWARE

The namesake martini glass is the obvious choice for the martini, but it's not the only one. I prefer to serve—and drink—my martini in a coupe glass. Following is a list of considerations for these and other options.

MARTINI GLASS

The cone-shaped bowl and long stem of the martini glass form an iconic silhouette recognized all over the world. The wide bowl allows for a greater appreciation of the aromatic gin, while the tall stem keeps your hand from warming up the ice-cold drink as you cradle it. One story holds that the glass was invented during Prohibition, with the wide bowl designed to allow for a quick toss of its contents should law enforcement suddenly appear. I like that mental image, but the truth is that the glass was introduced at a design exhibition in Paris in 1925, as a twist on the familiar coupe glass. Modern martini glasses are much bigger than the original 4-ounce (120 ml) model, with some holding as many as 10 ounces (300 ml). I find these giant glasses overrated, and I prefer to drink a couple of freshly made martinis in a row rather than to sip one monster-sized cocktail.

COUPE

Most people associate this wide-bowled stemmed glass with Champagne and other sparkling wines, but I don't limit it to bubbly drinks. I like to serve a martini in a coupe, as I prefer its size and shape to those of the signature glass. I have been avidly collecting vintage coupes from flea markets and antiques shops for years.

NICK & NORA GLASS

Another favorite choice for a martini is this one—a stemmed glass with a bell-shaped bowl that is wider than that of a wineglass but narrower than that of a martini glass or coupe. It's named for Nick and Nora Charles, the sophisticated, witty couple featured in Dashiell Hammett's novel *The Thin Man* (and the film series that followed).

THE TECHNIQUE

To shake or to stir? That is the question when it comes to the martini. The answer is one of personal preference. Many bartenders and martini lovers insist on stirring; others swear by shaking. (James Bond, as perhaps the best known example of the latter, always specified that his drink be "shaken, not stirred.") In terms of making the drink ice cold, there's little difference between the two methods. Shaking results in little shards of ice in your drink and a slightly cloudy appearance that clears with time. Stirred martinis are less prone to dilution. Again, the variation is slight.

Shaking seems more old-school, and there's a certain amount of pageantry involved in the process. In every airport bar I've been in, the martinis are shaken. Some claim that shaking "bruises" the gin, but I've never bought that line of argument. If you want your drink to be crystal clear, without even the tiniest piece of ice making its way through the strainer, you will probably prefer your martini stirred. Just take care not to stir (or shake, for that matter) for too long, lest the water from the ice begin to dilute the alcohol too much; thirty seconds is a good rule of thumb.

Your preference for dry or wet martinis will also influence the technique. The driest martinis contain only a whisper of vermouth. Many mixologists (myself included) achieve this by swirling a splash of vermouth around the bowl of the chilled glass, then tossing it out to make way for the ice-cold gin. (This is known as “rinsing” the glass.) If you are partial to a wet martini, pour the vermouth (and any other ingredients) into the shaker or mixing glass before chilling it with ice.

Your martini-making method is important, as are the ingredients and the equipment. However, there is no single factor more significant when serving and sipping a martini than its temperature—the colder, the better. The best bars in the world serve bracingly cold martinis, and once you’ve tasted one of those, you’ll want to re-create that experience at home. My preferred method is to keep the gin and glassware in the freezer, and the vermouth in the refrigerator. The result will be a drink that maintains its chilly temperature from start to finish, and that, for me, is perfection.

“Most experts will tell you that the bloom begins to fade from a martini as soon as it is first mixed, which may be pure subjectivism, but, in any drinking context, subjectivism is very important.”

—KINGSLEY AMIS,
Everyday Drinking

Sean Connery as James Bond in Dr. No, *1962*

THE

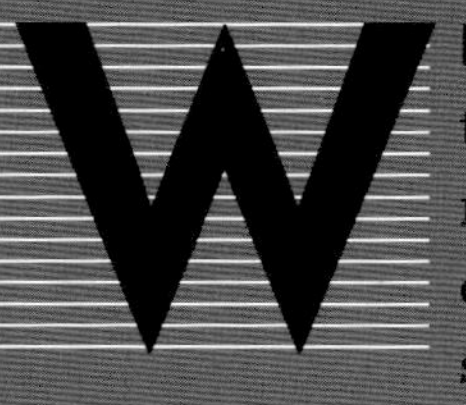

ITH AN EXCEPTION OR two, all the recipes in this book make one martini. Most are easy enough to double or scale up to serve more than one. (To make a big batch, see the recipe on page 73.)

The first recipe here is for my go-to martini, followed by other favorite riffs and interpretations. Some of the other examples, especially those that appear later in the book, are ones I have tried only once or twice, but I would be remiss not to share them. Nearly all of the components for each are easily accessible, but if you need to substitute one ingredient for another, feel free to do so. My hope is that you will not only enjoy making your way through the recipes that follow but will also learn to improvise along the way.

MARTINI
d'après Jean Droit
MARTINI
APÉRITIF
MARTINI & ROSSI

THE AUTHOR'S MARTINI

I always make my martini with gin, and garnish it with a twist of lemon (or, on *very* rare occasions, an olive, preferably pitted or pimento-stuffed). Because I like the cocktail near-frozen and prepared as quickly as possible (who likes to wait?), I keep the gin and my favorite coupe glass in the freezer. This technique guarantees a very cold, pure, undiluted martini with a lovely viscosity to the gin. The measurements below are included for guidance. I eyeball the amounts, and after you've made a few good martinis, chances are you will too.

- Splash of Noilly Prat dry vermouth
- 4 ounces (120 ml) London dry gin, preferably from the freezer
- Twist of lemon for garnish

Pour the vermouth into a frozen or well-chilled coupe glass, swirl the glass to coat it with vermouth, and toss out the excess. Pour the gin into the glass and garnish with the lemon twist.

THE AUTHOR'S "NOT SO DIRTY" MARTINI

I'm not a fan of a truly "dirty" martini (see page 135) because I find that proportion of olive brine excessive (and I don't like what it does to the color of the drink). Instead, I add just one bar spoon of green olive brine to "dust" the drink, not "dirty" it.

- Splash of Noilly Prat dry vermouth
- 4 ounces (120 ml) London dry gin, preferably from the freezer
- 1 bar spoon (about 1 teaspoon/ 5 ml) olive brine
- 2 pimento-stuffed olives for garnish

Pour the vermouth into a frozen or well-chilled glass of your choice, swirl the glass to coat it with vermouth, and pour out the excess. Combine the gin and brine in a cocktail shaker or mixing glass filled with ice. Shake or stir, as desired. Strain into the cold glass and garnish with the olives.

THE MARTINEZ

ANTIDOTE, ASHEVILLE, NORTH CAROLINA

Some say it all began with the Martinez. The quick story is that sometime around 1849, a Gold Rush–era miner walks into a bar in Martinez, California, northeast of San Francisco, and the bartender offers him a drink he calls the Martinez Special. The miner returns to San Francisco and spreads the word of the cocktail to other bartenders. The original drink is far less dry than the standard martini, with the sweet triple threat of Old Tom gin, sweet vermouth, and maraschino liqueur. I prefer this riff on the Martinez, served at Antidote in Asheville, North Carolina. The sweetness is there, but it's more considered than cloying, and it suits modern palates far better than the original.

- 2 ounces (60 ml) Chemist American gin
- 1 ounce (30 ml) Cocchi Vermouth di Torino
- 2 dashes Angostura bitters
- 1 Luxardo cherry for garnish

Combine the gin, vermouth, and bitters in a mixing glass filled with ice. Stir, then strain into a coupe. Garnish with the cherry.

THE CLASSIC MARTINI

Setting aside the story of the Martinez (page 46), many claim this as the formula that made the martini popular. Its ratio—one part gin to one part vermouth—makes it far less dry and gin-forward than most versions served today.

- 1½ ounces (45 ml) London dry gin
- 1½ ounces (45 ml) dry vermouth
- 3 dashes orange Angostura bitters (optional)
- An olive or a twist of lemon for garnish

Combine the gin, vermouth, and bitters, if using, in a cocktail shaker or mixing glass filled with ice. Shake or stir, as desired. Strain into a chilled martini glass. Garnish with the olive or lemon twist.

Bette Davis and Ronald Reagan in Dark Victory, *1939*

MONTGOMERY'S MARTINI

This driest of the dry variations on the classic martini is named for British field marshal Bernard Montgomery, who reportedly preferred the gin to outnumber the vermouth in his martini in about the same ratio as he liked to face his opponents in battle—fifteen to one! Ernest Hemingway liked his martini in this ratio too, and he mentioned the Montgomery in his 1950 novel *Across the River and into the Trees.*

- 5 ounces (150 ml) London dry gin
- ⅓ ounce (10 ml) dry vermouth, such as Noilly Prat extra dry
- Dash of orange bitters
- Strip of lemon peel for garnish

Combine the gin, vermouth, and bitters in a mixing glass filled with ice. Stir well, then strain into a glass of your choice and serve straight up. (Alternatively, strain it into a rocks glass filled with ice.) Garnish with the lemon peel.

“A well-crafted dirty martini should be viewed as a work of art and should be admired at least as often.”

—**MIKE BUICH,**

owner of Tadich Grill

"I was always told that good design is where smart 'form meets function.' The martini glass, high on stylish jet-set form, doesn't function terribly well as a cup. Anyone who's enjoyed more than two drinks in a sitting knows that a little spillage comes with the territory. So poor marks in the 'function' column.

"But the form! Here you have a glass straight out of George Jetson's cupboard filled with fuel worthy of a jet engine. Truth is, I reckon a proper gin martini is the smartest first-class ticket to cruising altitude. And when the seat belt sign comes off, it's almost always a great time."

—**MILES FISHER,**

founder of Bixby Coffee Roasters

Nobody needs it.
Everybody wants it.

DANTE

NEW YORK CITY

I'm a big fan and regular patron of Dante in New York City, both the legendary spot on MacDougal Street in Greenwich Village, which has been in operation since 1915, and the latest outpost, on Hudson Street in the West Village. They are famous for their multiple variations on the Negroni, but I like their inspired selection of martinis, as well (notably the three that follow, on pages 58, 61, and 62). The owner, Linden Pride, has become a great friend over the last several years, and I never pass up the opportunity to stop in and enjoy a cocktail in either location.

DANTE

THE UPSIDE-DOWN DIRTY GIBSON

This is Dante's nod to one of the forgotten classics of the American cocktail canon, the upside-down martini, which leans more heavily (you might even say aggressively) on the vermouth than on the gin. (Julia Child was known to be a fan of this inverted martini ratio.) Dante's version features equal parts of two vermouths, the classic Cinzano 1757 Extra Dry and the slightly sweeter Dolin Blanc, as well as Botanist, a floral-forward gin. A bit of pickled onion brine and a trace of wormwood bitters are added for good measure.

- 1 ounce (30 ml) Dolin Blanc vermouth
- 1 ounce (30 ml) Cinzano 1757 extra dry vermouth
- 1 ounce (30 ml) Botanist gin
- 1 bar spoon (about 1 teaspoon/ 5 ml) cocktail onion brine
- 2 dashes wormwood bitters (optional)
- 1 cocktail onion for garnish

Combine both vermouths, the gin, brine, and bitters, if using, in a mixing glass filled with ice. Stir, then strain into a coupe glass. Garnish with the onion.

DANTE

THE MARTINI TWIST

Don't let the long list of ingredients put you off—this is an amazing drink. It's complicated (gin *and* vodka *and* two vermouths!), but it's fresh, and dangerously good, with bright citrusy notes from the limoncello, citron vodka, and lemon bitters, and a little minerality from the Acqua Panna. I like the way Dante presents it, with the trio of garnishes in a bowl on the side, so you can take your pick and customize it as you wish.

- 1 bar spoon (about 1 teaspoon/ 5 ml) limoncello
- 1½ ounces (45 ml) Plymouth gin
- 1 ounce (30 ml) Absolut Citron vodka
- ½ ounce (15 ml) Alessio Vermouth Bianco
- ½ ounce (15 ml) Carpano dry vermouth
- 3 dashes lemon bitters
- 1 ounce (30 ml) Acqua Panna spring water
- Grapefruit coin, lemon knot, and lime knot for garnish

Pour the limoncello into a mixing glass filled with ice, then pour in the gin, vodka, both vermouths, the bitters, and water. Stir, then strain into a martini glass. Serve the garnishes on the side.

DANTE

THE OLIVETTE

As much as I love the experience of sitting at the bar at Dante, I also highly recommend their conveniently bottled cocktails, especially this one. It has trace floral notes from the St. Germain and a nice saltiness from the olive bitters.

- 1 ounce (30 ml) Bombay Sapphire gin
- 1 ounce (30 ml) Grey Goose vodka
- 1 ounce (30 ml) Noilly Prat dry vermouth
- ⅕ ounce (6 ml) St. Germain elderflower liqueur
- 1 dash olive bitters
- 1 ounce (30 ml) Acqua Panna water
- 1 large green olive, preferably Castelvetrano, for garnish

Combine the gin, vodka, vermouth, liqueur, bitters, and water in a cocktail shaker or mixing glass filled with ice. Shake or stir, as desired. Strain into a glass of your choice and garnish with the olive.

Olivette
Dante NYC

"It's a ritual, the Friday-night martini. My father's golf trophy, a small, silver cocktail shaker from the Shinnecock Hills 1962 Four Ball, taken from the freezer to pour out a single, generous, ice-cold martini. Heaven."

—BECKY LEWIS,

artists' agent

"The proper union of gin and vermouth is a great and sudden glory; it is one of the happiest marriages on earth and one of the shortest lived."

—**BERNARD DeVOTO,**

Harper's Magazine *(December 1949)*

THE ANCHOVY MARTINI

LA POSTA VECCHIA HOTEL, LADISPOLI, ITALY

When I was first offered this drink at the bar of La Posta Vecchia, a seaside hotel along the Roman coast, I was admittedly skeptical. Yet it had two things going for it: First, I *always* trust Italian bartenders, and second, I have a fondness for anything made with anchovies. The surprisingly delicious, savory cocktail is now among my favorites.

- 2 ounces (60 ml) Monkey 47 gin
- 1 ounce (30 ml) Italian dry vermouth
- 1 anchovy, rolled up and speared with a toothpick, for garnish

Combine the gin and vermouth in a mixing glass filled with ice, stir, then strain into an old-fashioned glass filled with ice. Garnish with the anchovy.

THE HARRY'S BAR MARTINI

HARRY'S BAR, VENICE AND NEW YORK CITY

To call me impatient is an understatement, and nothing is more frustrating than waiting an excessive amount of time for a drink to be set in front of me. Luckily, this is not a problem at Harry's Bar, where the martinis are premixed and poured into frozen short glasses in record time. Everything proceeds quickly, in one fell swoop. The only way to experience a delay is to hesitate on your choice of garnish. To make your own premixed martinis, simply scale up from the proportions below.

- 3 ounces (90 ml) London dry gin
- 1 bar spoon (about 1 teaspoon/ 5 ml) Martini & Rossi extra dry vermouth
- Twist of lemon or an olive for garnish

At least 30 minutes before serving, combine the gin and vermouth in a cocktail shaker and place in the freezer, along with a martini glass or glass of your choice. When ready to serve, shake the drink, then strain into the well-chilled glass. Garnish with the lemon twist or olive.

1323
HARR
HARRY

Harry's
Venice,

LEWIS HOUSE BATCHED MARTINIS

Serves 4

My family and I have made a tradition of Sunday dinners at our friends the Lewises' for some years now, and one of the highlights is the tray of cocktails served as soon as we walk in the door. Martinis are a house specialty. Steve uses his favorite gin, Tanqueray, and mixes the martinis in bulk, as we've found they go down like water. Fortunately, it's an easy taxi ride home at the end of the night.

- 16 ounces (480 ml) Tanqueray gin
- ½ ounce (15 ml) Dolin dry vermouth
- 4 lemon twists for garnish

At least a few hours ahead of serving, combine the gin and vermouth in a cocktail shaker. Place the shaker and four glasses in the freezer. Just before serving, add ice to the shaker and shake vigorously to break apart some of the cubes (Steve likes ice chips in his drink). Strain the martini mix into the frozen glasses, rub a lemon twist on each rim, and garnish the drink with it.

THE LIME MARTINI

In a nod to my dad's love of the gin and tonic with a slice of lime, I created this martini variation in his honor.

- 4 ounces (120 ml) London dry gin
- 1 ounce (30 ml) dry vermouth
- 1 ounce (30 ml) fresh lime juice
- Slice or twist of lime for garnish

Combine the gin, vermouth, and lime juice in a cocktail shaker or mixing glass filled with ice. Shake or stir, as desired. Strain into a coupe glass and garnish with the lime.

New York City

THE GIBSON

THE POLO BAR, NEW YORK CITY

Like the martini, the Gibson has a few conflicting origin stories. One version puts it at the Players in New York City, when the illustrator Charles Dana Gibson (creator of the "Gibson Girl" illustrations popular at the turn of the twentieth century) asked the bartender to riff on the martini. Others point to a San Francisco businessman and member of the Bohemian Club, Walter D. K. Gibson, who asked for onions in his drink because he believed they could help prevent the common cold. Whatever the case may be, the Gibson is a nice, more subtle alternative to the classic martini, since cocktail onions are not quite as assertive as olives or lemon. When the urge for a Gibson strikes me, I head straight to the Polo Bar in New York City, the perfect place to enjoy one.

- 2¼ ounces (65 ml) London dry gin
- ¾ ounce (20 ml) dry vermouth
- Cocktail onions for garnish

Combine the gin and vermouth in a cocktail shaker or mixing glass filled with ice. Shake or stir, as desired, then pour into a coupe or glass of your choice. Garnish with a few cocktail onions.

THE RAMP GIBSON

WM BROWN FARM, NEW YORK

Each spring, my family and I eagerly await the arrival of ramps, the wild alliums that grow all over the rocky southern slopes of our farm in upstate New York. We harvest piles of them, then I get to work cleaning and cooking them. One of my favorite things to do is to quick-pickle the ramp bulbs. Substituting a pickled ramp for the usual cocktail onion, with a little of the ramp brine added to the mix, makes a delightful seasonal variation on the classic Gibson.

- 4 ounces (120 ml) London dry gin, preferably from the freezer
- Splash of dry vermouth, such as Dolin
- 1 Pickled Ramp (recipe follows) for garnish, plus 2 bar spoons (about 2 teaspoons/10 ml) of the brine

Combine the gin, vermouth, and brine in a cocktail shaker or mixing glass filled with ice. Shake or stir, as desired. Strain into a coupe glass. Garnish with the pickled ramp.

(continued)

DRY
DOLIN
VERMOUTH

PICKLED RAMPS

- 2 quarts (2 L) warm water
- ½ cup (120 g) kosher salt
- 1½ pounds (680 g) ramps, bulbs trimmed, leaves reserved for another use (they make a great pesto)
- 2 cups (480 ml) malt vinegar
- 2 tablespoons dark brown sugar
- 1 teaspoon black peppercorns
- 1 teaspoon whole allspice berries
- ¼ teaspoon hot pepper flakes
- 1 bay leaf

Pour 1 quart (1 L) of the water into a large bowl, add ¼ cup (60 g) of the salt, and stir to dissolve. Add the ramp bulbs and let stand for 1 hour, then drain.

Return the ramp bulbs to the bowl. Dissolve the remaining ¼ cup (60 g) salt in the remaining 1 quart (1 L) water and pour over the ramp bulbs.

Meanwhile, combine the vinegar, brown sugar, peppercorns, allspice berries, hot pepper flakes, and bay leaf in a nonreactive saucepan and bring to a boil, stirring to dissolve the sugar. Remove from the heat and let the brine cool.

Using a slotted spoon, layer the ramps in a quart-size (1 L) glass jar and cover with the cooled brine. Refrigerate the ramps for a few days before using; they should keep for 3 months or more in the refrigerator.

"Mixing a martini before breakfast takes some getting used to, but when that cocktail shaker comes out of the freezer in the evening, it all makes sense."

—**STEPHEN LEWIS,**
photographer

Photographer Dewey Nicks's Bel Air, California, home

THE GIMLET

ANTIDOTE, ASHEVILLE, NORTH CAROLINA

Cocktail historians date this drink back to the nineteenth century, when strong ("Navy strength"!) gin was mixed with Rose's lime juice cordial and served to British sailors to ward off scurvy. On a more personal level, this traditional sour was my gateway to the martini, with its lime and sugar tempering the bite of the gin. In my youth, I lacked the confidence (and the palate) to understand what made a martini great—the gin—so I ordered gimlets with abandon until age and experience changed my ways.

- 2½ ounces (75 ml) London dry gin
- ¼ ounce (7 ml) fresh lime juice
- ½ ounce (15 ml) Simple Syrup (recipe follows)
- Slice of lime for garnish

Combine the gin, lime juice, and simple syrup in a mixing glass filled with ice. Stir vigorously with a bar spoon until very cold. Strain into a chilled glass of your choice, filled with ice or without, depending on your preference. Garnish with the lime slice.

SIMPLE SYRUP

- 1 cup (200 g) sugar
- 1 cup (240 ml) water

Combine the sugar and water in a saucepan and bring to a simmer, swirling the pan or stirring until the sugar dissolves. Let the syrup cool completely, then store it in an airtight container in the refrigerator for up to a month.

THE PICKLED MARTINI

This cocktail is rooted in the world of the Gibson (page 79) but serves as an especially savory, non-citrusy alternative to the standard martini. I include it—and make one myself sometimes—due to the simple fact that, believe it or not, you can on occasion get bored with the classic martini. The cornichon brine is a nice flavor addition.

- 3 ounces (90 ml) London dry gin
- ¾ ounce (20 ml) dry vermouth
- 1 bar spoon (about 1 teaspoon/5 ml) cornichon brine
- Cornichons for garnish

Combine the gin, vermouth, and brine in a cocktail shaker or mixing glass filled with ice. Shake or stir, as desired, then strain into a coupe glass. Garnish with the cornichons.

STAND
8 YEARS

Alan Alda as Hawkeye Pierce in M*A*S*H, *1974*

RUSS & DAUGHTERS
CAFE
SINCE 1914

RUSS & DAUGHTERS CAFE

NEW YORK CITY

I am a die-hard fan of Russ & Daughters, the smoked-fish emporium on Manhattan's Lower East Side now run by the fourth generation of the Russ family. Everything on the menu is inspired by the history of the neighborhood, home to Jewish immigrants from eastern Europe since the early nineteenth century. When the family (finally!) opened a sit-down version of their "appetizing" shop, I was happy to see they had incorporated some of the traditional ingredients and inspirations of their menu into their bar offerings. The three that follow (on pages 96, 99, and 100) are my favorites, each a delicious, innovative, and highly personal take on the classic martini.

RUSS & DAUGHTERS CAFE

THE SMOKED

I like how this recipe transfers one of the key flavors of Russ & Daughters—smoke—from the appetizing platter to the cocktail glass. The glass is rinsed with Laphroaig, an especially smoky Scotch, then filled with a combination of spirits, chief among them Perry's Tot "Navy Strength" gin. Distilled in Brooklyn, the gin is named for an early commandant of its historic Navy Yard (now home to another Russ & Daughters Cafe).

- Splash of Laphroaig 10-year Scotch
- 1 ounce (30 ml) Perry's Tot gin
- ½ ounce (15 ml) Belvedere vodka
- ½ ounce (15 ml) Cocchi Americano
- ½ ounce (15 ml) Lillet Blanc

Pour the Scotch into a chilled coupe glass, swirl to coat the glass, and toss out the excess. Combine the gin, vodka, Cocchi, and Lillet in a mixing glass filled with ice and stir with a bar spoon. Strain into the chilled coupe.

HERRING
PLATTERS
SHARED
EGGS
ALL THE TIME
served
LOX, EGGS & ONIONS | 18
with TOASTED SHISSEL RYE
STURGEON, EGGS & ONIONS | 22
with TOASTED PUMPERNICKEL
LOWER SUNNY SIDE | 19
EGGS BENNY | 20
"Ess gezinter hayt."
Eat in good health.
-Yiddish idiom

RUSS & DAUGHTERS CAFE

THE LOWER EAST SIDE

Consider this riff on the martini an homage to the cuisine of the neighborhood the Russ family has called home for more than a hundred years. Cucumber and dill, both traditional garnishes for the cafe's famous appetizing platters, flavor a cocktail of gin, lime juice, and simple syrup.

- 4 slices cucumber
- A healthy pinch of fresh dill fronds, plus a small sprig for garnish
- ¾ ounce (20 ml) fresh lime juice
- ¾ ounce (20 ml) Simple Syrup (page 87)
- 2 ounces (60 ml) Tanqueray gin

Muddle the cucumber slices and the dill fronds in the bottom of a cocktail shaker. Add the lime juice, simple syrup, gin, and ice and shake well (meaning very hard). Double-strain (through the shaker and then a fine-mesh sieve) into a chilled coupe glass and garnish with the sprig of dill.

RUSS & DAUGHTERS CAFE

THE BREAK-FAST

This take on the martini, which includes elements of a classic sour cocktail (citrus juice, simple syrup, and egg white), is named for the practice of breaking the fast on Yom Kippur, the holiest day of the Jewish year. The addition of bitter orange jam may seem quirky, but it dates back at least as far as 1930, when a recipe for a marmalade cocktail was included in *The Savoy Cocktail Book* (see page 105). Raw egg whites, which help emulsify the ingredients, have the potential to carry foodborne illness, so enjoy with caution (or use powdered pasteurized egg whites).

- Splash of Pernod absinthe
- 1 large (30 g) egg white
- 2 ounces (60 ml) Beefeater gin
- ¾ ounce (20 ml) fresh lemon juice
- ½ ounce (15 ml) Simple Syrup (page 87)
- 1 bar spoon (about 1 teaspoon/ 5 ml) bitter orange jam
- Angostura bitters for garnish

Pour the absinthe into a chilled coupe glass, swirl to coat the glass, and toss out the excess. Place the egg white in the bottom of a cocktail shaker. Add the gin, lemon juice, simple syrup, and jam to the top half of the shaker, then combine the two parts and dry-shake (no ice) for at least 30 seconds. Add ice and shake briefly to chill. (There should be a thick froth; if not, keep shaking.) Strain into the chilled coupe. Add 3 drops of bitters on top of the foam, then drag a toothpick or skewer through them to make a fishtail design.

From left to right: Ann Warner, Lili Damita, Marlene Dietrich, Jack Warner, and Errol Flynn, 1938

The Savoy Cocktail Book

THE SAVOY

The three recipes on the following page are from *The Savoy Cocktail Book,* an early-twentieth-century tome filled with many of the most classic cocktail recipes. I include these examples to illustrate the versatility and adaptability of the martini. By playing with the proportions and slightly varying the essential components, you can produce martinis with a range of flavors and characteristics along the dry-to-sweet spectrum. Consider this the "have it your way" approach.

THE SAVOY

DRY

- 2 ounces (60 ml) London dry gin
- 1 ounce (30 ml) French dry vermouth
- Strip of lemon peel or an olive for garnish

Combine the gin and vermouth in a cocktail shaker or mixing glass filled with ice. Shake or stir, as desired. Strain into a coupe glass. Garnish with the lemon or olive.

MEDIUM

- 1½ ounces (45 ml) London dry gin
- ¾ ounce (20 ml) French dry vermouth
- ¾ ounce (20 ml) Italian sweet vermouth
- Strip of lemon peel or an olive for garnish

Combine the gin and both vermouths in a cocktail shaker or mixing glass filled with ice. Shake or stir, as desired. Strain into a coupe glass. Garnish with the lemon or olive.

SWEET

- 2 ounces (60 ml) London dry gin
- 1 ounce (30 ml) Italian sweet vermouth
- Strip of lemon peel or an olive for garnish

Combine the gin and vermouth in a cocktail shaker or mixing glass filled with ice. Shake or stir, as desired. Strain into a coupe glass. Garnish with the lemon or olive.

the ODEON

THE CUCUMBER MARTINI

THE ODEON, NEW YORK CITY

When I first moved to New York City in 1990, nothing brought to life the age of Jay McInerney's *Bright Lights, Big City* more than an evening at the bar of the Odeon in TriBeCa. Some of my young-adult life's greatest moments happened there (including the first dinner with my wife). I still go there to get my nostalgic fix, often at the bar and most likely with a martini.

- 5 slices cucumber
- 2 ounces (60 ml) Hendrick's gin, preferably from the freezer
- ¾ ounce (20 ml) dry vermouth, preferably Dolin
- ½ ounce (15 ml) St. Germain elderflower liqueur

Muddle 4 of the cucumber slices in the bottom of a cocktail shaker. Fill the shaker with ice, add the gin, vermouth, and liqueur, and shake. Strain into a chilled martini glass and garnish with the remaining cucumber slice.

"The Martini is the Mount Everest of cocktails. If it were a painter, it would be Picasso; if it were a car, it would be a Ferrari; if it were a singer, it would be Sinatra. Drinking one is a fabulous way to end a tough day, and an even better way to begin a perfect evening."

—**NATHAN WOODEN,**

wine and spirits writer and restaurant consultant

"A true martini is a gin martini. When you order a martini, the bartender should automatically make you one using gin. It should only be if you say, 'Can I have a vodka martini?' that they should assume you want vodka with a bit of vermouth and an olive or twist in a beautiful triangular-shaped glass."

—**PAUL FEIG,**

Hollywood director, writer, and producer, and creator of Artingstall's Brilliant London Dry Gin

London

Dukes Bar
1908

DUKES BAR

LONDON

Alessandro Palazzi, the current bar manager of the famed Dukes in London's Mayfair neighborhood, is an undisputed master of his craft. He's known the world over for his signature drinks—the Vesper (page 116) and the namesake Dukes martini (page 119)—as well as the tableside service, which is, in my opinion, second to none in the world.

DUKES BAR

THE VESPER

This famously appealing drink is so lethal that Dukes imposed a two-Vesper limit at the bar, which is strictly enforced at all times. The cocktail was very much inspired by author Ian Fleming, a patron of Dukes, and his famous character, James Bond, who orders the drink in the 1953 novel *Casino Royale*. It's named in honor of Bond's double-agent girlfriend, Vesper Lynd. Originally the Vesper was made with Kina Lillet, vodka, gin, and bitters, but these days, Dukes uses Sacred Spirits brand vermouth in place of Kina Lillet, which is no longer available.

- 4 dashes Angostura bitters
- 2½ ounces (75 ml) No. 3 London dry gin, preferably from the freezer
- 1 ounce (30 ml) Polish vodka, preferably from the freezer
- ⅓ ounce (10 ml) Sacred Spirits English Amber vermouth, preferably from the freezer
- Twist of orange, preferably organic, for garnish

Add the bitters to a frozen martini glass. Combine the gin, vodka, and vermouth in a cocktail shaker filled with ice. Shake, then strain into the glass and garnish with the orange twist.

No 3
LONDON DRY
POTOCKI
Dukes Bar
1908

DUKES BAR

THE DUKES MARTINI

This five-shot house martini packs a memorable punch. Bar manager Alessandro Palazzi suggests that you take your time and linger over it. The martini is made tableside (Dukes claims to be the first establishment to have done so, a practice that has since been copied by many), and the vermouth is tossed right onto the carpet (Palazzi's signature touch) after it's used to rinse the glass. As with the Vesper, Dukes strictly—and wisely—limits patrons to two.

- Splash of Sacred Spirits English dry vermouth
- 5 ounces (150 ml) London dry gin (Palazzi uses No. 3, Plymouth, or Sacred Spirits), preferably from the freezer
- Twist of lemon, preferably organic, for garnish

Pour a few drops of vermouth into a frozen martini glass. Swirl to rinse, then toss the vermouth over your shoulder. Pour the frozen gin into the glass. Express the lemon twist over the drink, then garnish the martini with it.

"One martini for me a day keeps the doctor away."

—ALESSANDRO PALAZZI,

bar manager at Dukes Bar, London

"A well-made Martini or Gibson, correctly chilled and nicely served, has been more often my true friend than any two-legged creature."

—M. F. K. FISHER,

"To the Gibson and Beyond,"
The Atlantic *(January 1949)*

THE VESPER ALTERNATIVE

GRAND HOTEL VESUVIO, NAPLES, ITALY

This variation comes from one of my favorite barkeepers, Antonio at the Grand Hotel Vesuvio. It is gin-forward, but with a small measure of vodka and traces of Sicilian dessert wine and China Martini (an Italian aperitif made by Martini & Rossi and flavored with cinchona bark and a blend of herbs and spices).

- 2¼ ounces (65 ml) Gordon's gin
- ¾ ounce (20 ml) vodka
- ¼ ounce (7 ml) Sicilian dessert wine
- 1 bar spoon (about 1 teaspoon/ 5 ml) China Martini
- Twist of lemon for garnish

Combine the gin, vodka, dessert wine, and China Martini in a cocktail shaker or mixing glass filled with ice. Stir or shake, as desired. Strain into a glass of your choice and garnish with the lemon twist.

“What sane man of my generation doesn’t love James Bond? I had my first martini at the Plaza’s Oak Room after seeing an early Bond film. I still enjoy this luxury, now with Chopin vodka with a few droplets of Yzaguirre vermouth. That first sip . . .”

—**KEN ARETSKY,**

restaurateur

Pierce Brosnan as James Bond in Die Another Day, *2002*

THE POET'S DREAM

This inspired martini comes from my old friend Damon Boelte, formerly the bar manager at Prime Meats in Carroll Gardens, Brooklyn, and now the proprietor of Grand Army in nearby Park Slope. The hint of Bénédictine liqueur brings barely detectable floral and herbaceous notes that don't get in the way of the gin.

- 2 ounces (60 ml) London dry gin
- ¾ ounce (20 ml) dry vermouth
- ¼ ounce (7 ml) Bénédictine
- Twist of lemon for garnish

Combine the gin, vermouth, and liqueur in a cocktail shaker filled with ice. Shake, then strain into a coupe glass. Garnish with the lemon twist.

THE MARGUERITE

Damon Boelte's riff on this early version of a dry martini features artisanal Botanist gin, which is made on the Scottish isle of Islay and flavored with twenty-two hand-foraged local botanicals. Its highly complex, layered flavor profile works well in this cocktail, marked by a citrusy finish.

- 2 ounces (60 ml) Botanist gin
- 1 ounce (30 ml) dry vermouth
- Dash of orange bitters
- Twist of lemon for garnish

Combine the gin, vermouth, and bitters in a cocktail shaker filled with ice. Shake, then strain into a glass of your choice. Express the lemon twist over the drink, then garnish the martini with it.

BIX'S MARTINI

BIX, SAN FRANCISCO

A San Francisco institution, this dreamy, jazzy place down an alley in Jackson Square is named for its proprietor, Doug "Bix" Biederbeck. It's famous for its martini, which is always served in a classic Nick & Nora glass.

- 3½ ounces (105 ml) Gordon's gin
- ½ ounce (15 ml) Dolin dry vermouth
- 1 or 2 olives or cocktail onions or a twist of lemon for garnish

Combine the gin and vermouth in a cocktail shaker or mixing glass filled with ice. Shake or stir, as desired. Strain into a Nick & Nora glass. Garnish with the olives, onions, or lemon twist.

HERE

WARNERS
RALPH THOMAS
VOCAL STUDIOS
WARNERS
SECURITY
EQUITABLE BLDG
PANTAGES

MICHAEL BUICH

THE DIRTY MARTINI

TADICH GRILL, SAN FRANCISCO

As a rule, I keep my martini simple and straightforward. I like it crystal clear, direct, dry, and *clean*. That said, I recognize that the so-called dirty variation has won legions of fans over many years, FDR among them. President Roosevelt was a big proponent of the cocktail hour, mixing the drinks himself for guests (including Stalin, to whom he famously served a martini when the Allied leaders met in Tehran in 1943). Dirty martinis are wildly popular today. On occasion, I've been known to order one at Bemelmans Bar at the Carlyle Hotel in New York City, or at Tadich Grill in San Francisco.

- 2 ounces (60 ml) London dry gin
- ½ ounce (15 ml) dry vermouth
- ½ ounce (15 ml) olive brine
- Olives for garnish (the more, the dirtier)

Combine the gin, vermouth, and brine in a cocktail shaker or mixing glass filled with ice. Shake or stir, as desired. Strain into a martini glass and garnish with the olives.

ESTABLISHED 1849
TADICH
GRILL
242
Tad

Exterior of the Tadich Grill, San Francisco, California

THE FILTHY MARTINI

MELFI'S, CHARLESTON, SOUTH CAROLINA

If the dirty martini feels a bit too clean for you, try this version inspired by Melfi's in Charleston, which takes the theme a step further with a blue cheese–stuffed olive garnish. The drink is open to interpretation; add as much or as little olive brine or as many olives as you like, depending on just how filthy you want it (or how hungry you are).

- 3 ounces (90 ml) London dry gin
- ¾ ounce (20 ml) dry vermouth
- Splash of olive brine
- Blue cheese–stuffed olives for garnish

Combine the gin, vermouth, and brine in a cocktail shaker or mixing glass filled with ice. Shake or stir, as desired. Strain into a coupe glass and garnish with the stuffed olives.

THE OLIO MARTINI

FRANKS WINE BAR, BROOKLYN, NEW YORK

Named for its distinctive olive oil garnish, this martini comes from my friends Frank Castronovo and Frank Falcinelli (aka "The Franks") of Brooklyn restaurant fame. They're the duo behind Frankies 457 Spuntino, Franks Wine Bar, F&F Pizzeria, and the late, great Prime Meats. They use salt bitters (a couple dashes' worth) in this martini, but because those can be hard to find, I substitute a pinch of flaky sea salt.

- 2 ounces (60 ml) Plymouth gin
- 1 ounce (30 ml) Dolin Blanc vermouth
- Pinch of sea salt or kosher salt
- Strip of lemon peel
- Extra-virgin olive oil for garnish

Combine the gin, vermouth, and salt in a cocktail shaker or mixing glass filled with ice. Shake or stir, as desired. Rub the lemon peel around the rim of a coupe glass and discard. Strain the drink into the glass and garnish with a drop of olive oil. (A bottle with a spout is best to achieve the floating disc of oil.)

"Each house we have lived in has had a cocktail that seemed to be a perfect fit. For the sexy midcentury modern in Bel Air, it was an icy vodka martini. A quick swirl of vermouth in a chilled glass, Ketel One with shimmering flecks of ice poured from a steel shaker so cold that it's hard to hold, finished with a single green olive. Perfection."

—**DEWEY NICKS,**
photographer

"From the Gibson to the classic dirty, there are a million different ways to whip up a martini, but my favorite of all the variations is the espresso martini. It's my preferred after-dinner indulgence to carry me into the night."

—ZACHARY WEISS,

brand consultant and editor

Sant

THE ESPRESSO MARTINI

SANT AMBROEUS, NEW YORK CITY

An espresso martini is only as good as the espresso it's made with. No amount of creamy coffee liqueurs or other ingredients can hide the taste of a poorly pulled shot. What I like about the Sant Ambroeus version of the drink is that it starts with a well-chilled shot of their perfect espresso. The other additions are surprising: vanilla vodka; Tuaca, an Italian brandy liqueur flavored with Mediterranean citrus; and Galliano, the famously yellow, sweet, herbal liqueur. Ordinarily I would not find the combination of those ingredients at all appealing. Yet thanks to the perfect bitterness of their espresso, what you get instead is a wonderfully balanced, coffee-forward, delicious martini.

- 1½ ounces (45 ml) espresso, chilled
- 2 ounces (60 ml) vanilla vodka
- ½ ounce (15 ml) Tuaca
- 1½ ounces (45 ml) Galliano
- 3 coffee beans for garnish

Combine the espresso, vodka, and both liqueurs in a cocktail shaker filled with ice. Shake vigorously and strain into a coupe or glass of your choice. Garnish with the coffee beans.

Dean Martin, Hollywood, California, 1961

THE SNACKS

I like to pair my martinis with all manner of salty, savory snacks—from a bowl of crunchy Lay's potato chips to a nice tin of caviar. (I like Petrossian.) The key is to keep it uncomplicated, like the drink itself.

- Potato chips, by themselves or with sour cream and onion dip
- Salted nuts
- An aged cheese, such as Manchego
- Triscuits with cheese (I like Kaukauna spreadable cheese from Wisconsin)
- Cheddar Goldfish crackers or Cheez-Its
- Popcorn
- Crudités (the ones at Tower Bar in Los Angeles are my gold standard), with or without a creamy dip
- Finger-sized grilled cheese sandwiches, like the ones at Harry's Bar in Venice
- Chex Mix
- Caviar (from Osetra to paddlefish and everything in between—whatever you can afford), with blini, cucumber slices, or, of course, potato chips

Beefeater® gin. Distilled and bottled in London by the Burrough family. The only gin ever to be honored with the Queen's Award to industry.

The Gin of England

THE BLACK BOOK

Following is a list of my absolute favorite places in which to order a martini or two. I don't generally recommend bars or restaurants I haven't visited, bartenders I've never met, or cocktails I've never tasted, but I remain open to the recommendations of fellow martini enthusiasts. If I'm missing out on a fantastic martini or an excellent spot in which to enjoy one, please don't hesitate to let me know. I'm always eager to try something new.

France

Bar Hemingway
Ritz Paris
15 Place Vendôme
Paris
+33 1 43 16 33 74
ritzparis.com/en-GB
/fine-dining-paris
/bar-hemingway

Cravan
17 Rue Jean de la Fontaine
Paris
+33 1 40 50 14 30
@cravanparis

Le Bar
Four Seasons Hotel George V
31 Avenue George V
Paris
+33 1 49 52 70 06
fourseasons.com/paris
/dining/lounges/le_bar

Italy

Grand Hotel Vesuvio
Via Partenope 45
Naples
+39 081 764 0044
vesuvio.it/en/bar

Harry's Bar
San Marco 1323
Venice
+39 041 52 85 777
cipriani.com/us/harrys-bar

La Posta Vecchia Hotel
Via Palo Laziale
00055 Ladispoli
+39 06 9949501
postavecchiahotel.com/en/dining/the-cesar.html

The United Kingdom

Dukes Bar
35 St. James's Place
London
+44 20 7491 4840
dukeshotel.com/dukes-bar

The United States

Antidote at Chemist Spirits
151 Coxe Avenue
Asheville, North Carolina
828-263-6943
antidote.bar

Aretsky's Patroon
160 East 46th Street
New York City
212-883-7373
aretskyspatroon.com

Bemelmans Bar
The Carlyle Hotel
35 East 76th Street
New York City
212-570-7120
rosewoodhotels.com/en/the-carlyle-new-york/dining/bemelmans-bar

Bix
56 Gold Street
San Francisco
415-433-6300
bixrestaurant.com

Bobby Van's Steakhouse
JFK Airport
Terminal 8
Queens, New York
718-553-2100
bobbyvans.com/steakhouse/JFK

Cipriani Downtown
376 West Broadway
New York City
212-343-0999
cipriani.com/us/cipriani-downtown-ny

Coltivare
3320 White Oak Drive
Houston
713-637-4095
agricolehospitality.com/coltivare

Dante
79-81 MacDougal Street
New York City
212-982-5275
dante-nyc.com

Franks Wine Bar
465 Court Street
Brooklyn, New York
718-254-0327
frankswinebar.com

Grand Army
336 State Street
Brooklyn, New York
718-643-1503
grandarmybar.com

Harry Cipriani
The Sherry-Netherland Hotel
781 Fifth Avenue
New York City
212-753-5566
cipriani.com/us/harry-cipriani-ny

Keens Steakhouse
72 West 36th Street
New York City
212-947-3636
keens.com

King Cole Bar
The St. Regis New York
2 East 55th Street
New York City
212-753-4500
marriott.com/hotels/hotel-information/restaurant/details/nycxr-the-st-regis-new-york/6359135

Knickerbocker Bar & Grill
33 University Place
New York City
212-228-8490
knickerbockerbarandgrill.com

La Mercerie
53 Howard Street
New York City
212-852-9097
lamerceriecafe.com

Melfi's
721 King Street
Charleston, South Carolina
843-513-0307
eatatmelfis.com

The Odeon
145 West Broadway
New York City
212-233-0507
theodeonrestaurant.com

The Polo Bar
1 East 55th Street
New York City
212-207-8562
ralphlauren.com/global-polo-bar

The Polo Lounge
The Beverly Hills Hotel
9641 Sunset Boulevard
Beverly Hills
310-887-2777
dorchestercollection.com/en/los-angeles/the-beverly-hills-hotel/restaurants-bars/the-polo-lounge

Quince
470 Pacific Avenue
San Francisco
415-775-8500
quincerestaurant.com

Raoul's
180 Prince Street
New York City
212-966-3518
raouls.com

Russ & Daughters Cafe
127 Orchard Street
New York City
212-475-4880
russanddaughterscafe.com

Sant Ambroeus
265 Lafayette Street
New York City
212-966-2770
santambroeus.com/restaurant-sant-ambroeus-soho

Tadich Grill
240 California Street
San Francisco
415-391-1849
tadichgrillsf.com

The Tower Bar
Sunset Tower Hotel
8358 Sunset Boulevard
West Hollywood
323-848-6677
sunsettowerhotel.com/restaurants-and-bar/tower-bar

AFTERWORD

I am always surprised when a cocktail with so few ingredients—the holy trinity of cold gin, dry vermouth, and garnish—and such a relatively straightforward preparation ends up undrinkable. That being said, when prepared with thoughtfulness and care, the martini is perfection in a glass. It's an adult drink for sure: serious, sophisticated, sexy, with a bit of Old Hollywood romance thrown in. The martini warrants respect, and often tastes better when one is in the company of others (though I've certainly enjoyed many a martini alone). And I seem to enjoy martinis best when I'm wearing a tuxedo.

ACKNOWLEDGMENTS

I would like to thank my favorite drinking partner, Yolanda Edwards, who helped in the research of this book! My daughter, Clara, who, I imagine, will grow to love these concoctions. Thanks also to Ken Aretsky, Edmund Barr, BeccaPR, Damon Boelte, Mike Buich, Frank Castronovo, Kate Cunningham, Darnell Dodson, Frank Falcinelli, Niki Russ Federman, Matthew Karl Gale, Gary Harrison, Stephen Lewis, Dewey Nicks, Alessandro Palazzi, Jay Poblador, Linden Pride, Brooks Reitz, Jennifer Schwartz, Josh Russ Tupper—and Ellen Morrissey, for her calm demeanor, expert advice, and ability to keep me on track with this book's content and words. I raise my glass to my incredibly fab Artisan team: my publisher, Lia Ronnen; editor, Shoshana Gutmajer; Elise Ramsbottom; Suet Chong; Nina Simoneaux; Sibylle Kazeroid; Barbara Peragine; Nancy Murray; Allison McGeehon; and Theresa Collier.

PHOTOGRAPHY CREDITS

Page 6: Neil Baylis/Alamy Stock Photo
Page 10: Gary Harrison
Page 14: 20th Century Fox Film Corp. TM & Copyright/ Courtesy: Everett Collection
Page 19: f8 archive/Alamy Stock Photo
Page 24: Image Courtesy of The Advertising Archives
Page 28: Francis Miller/The LIFE Picture Collection via Getty Images
Page 38: Everett Collection
Page 41: Image Courtesy of The Advertising Archives
Pages 50–51: Everett Collection
Page 56: Riley Sheehey
Page 64: Stephen Lewis
Pages 70–71: Leonardo Cendamo/Getty Images
Pages 76–77: Elliott Erwitt/Magnum Photos
Pages 84–85: Edmund Barr
Pages 90–91: 20th Century Fox Television. All Rights reserved./Courtesy Everett Collection
Page 92: Charles Phelps Cushing/ClassicStock/Getty Images
Page 93: Yolanda Edwards
Page 94: Courtesy of Russ & Daughters Cafe
Pages 102–103: PictureLux/The Hollywood Archive/Alamy Stock Photo
Pages 112–113: Tony Eyles/Mirrorpix/Getty Images
Page 114: Gary Harrison
Page 117: Gary Harrison
Page 125: Album/Alamy Stock Photo
Page 133: Ralph Crane/The LIFE Picture Collection via Getty Images
Pages 146–147: Sid Avery/mptvimages.com
Page 160: Clara Hranek

INDEX

Note: Page numbers in *italics* refer to illustrations.

Matt Hranek is the author of *A Man & His Watch*, *A Man & His Car*, and *The Negroni*. He's the founder and editor of *Wm Brown*, a men's lifestyle magazine. Some of his longest friendships have started with a well-made drink at a favorite bar. He and his family divide their time between Brooklyn and the Wm Brown Farm in upstate New York. Find him on Instagram at @wmbrownproject.